ERIK SATIE
Deux Gymnopédies

Orchestrated by
Claude Debussy

Study Score
Partitur

SERENISSIMA MUSIC, INC.

PREFACE

Satie composed his *Trois Gymnopédies* between February and April of 1888. The set of piano pieces was published later that year by the composer himself and subsequently by the Paris firm E. Baudoux et Cie. Though the *Gymnopédies* have become Satie's most famous and beloved work worldwide in the ensuing decades, they were still relatively unknown in late 1896 when Satie's fellow composer Claude Debussy (1862-1918) gave a brilliant impromptu performance during a social gathering at the Paris home of the Swiss conductor Gustave Doret (1866-1943) with the composer in attendance. Doret was so taken with the *Gymnopédies* that he immediately suggested that Debussy prepare an orchestral setting for an upcoming concert of the Société Nationale. Satie readily agreed to this arrangement, presumably in deference to Debussy's greater experience in orchestration at that time. Though Debussy and Satie had first met five years earlier, it was Debussy's outstanding introduction of the *Gymnopédies* to such an important Paris audience that led to their friendship, which endured to Debussy's death in 1918.

For reasons which remain obscure, Debussy elected to include only two of the three pieces (Nos. 1 and 3) whose order was reversed for his orchestral setting. Thus the *Deux Gymnopédies* received its premiere at the concert presented by the Société Nationale on February 20th, 1897 under the Doret's direction. Debussy's orchestration was published by Baudoux later the same year. Debussy conducted the work himself for the first time much later – on March 25, 1911 at a concert of the Cercle Musical. By this time, Satie was at last becoming known as a composer in his own right, thanks in part to the popularity of Debussy's orchestral setting of these early piano pieces.

While often quite disdainful of impresionist orchestral writing later in life, Satie always excepted Debussy from the criticism and praised the sensitive treatment given by his friend to the *Gymnopédies*.

The present edition is based upon the following sources:

I. The full score published by E. Baudoux in 1897, plate number E. B. et Cie. 403; 7 pages. Baudoux was absorbed by the newly-formed Rouart-Lerolle in 1905, which was in turn absorbed by Salabert in 1941. Thus there are several later printings bearing the name of the successor firms. In addition, this score has been reprinted in the United States over the years by Broude Brothers, Ltd., Luck's Music, Inc. and E. F. Kalmus, Inc.

II. The original piano version, which was first issued by the composer in 1888 and subsequently re-issued by Baudoux at about the same time as the full score (I). In addition to numerous printings over the years by the successor firms mentioned above, the work has been reprinted extensively in the United States and elsewhere, most recently in a collection of Satie's piano works issued by Dover.

The primary source of the present edition is the Baudoux full score, which despite an overall layout that can be confusing in places, is reasonably accurate in terms of being consistent with the composer's notation in the original piano version of the two pieces orchestrated. The one area where Debussy was slightly careless in transcribing his friend's music lies in his frequent omission of Satie's crescendo and diminuendo hairpins which appear above the melodic line in the original piano score. For the present edition, Satie's carefully notated hairpins have been restored. Editorial dynamics are enclosed in brackets in the few places where they have been added. Both score and parts for this edition have been newly engraved, with a much more spacious layout designed to facilitate performance.

Carl Simpson
Summer, 2004

Deux Gymnopédies
1ere Gymnopédie
(No. 3 in the Piano original)

ERIK SATIE
(1866-1925)
Orchestrated by Claude Debussy
edited by Carl Simpson

2ème Gymnopédie

(No. 1 in the Piano original)

* "frappez avec unde baguette de timbale"

SERENISSIMA MUSIC, INC.

Serenissima publications include digitally-enhanced reprints of authoritative editions for standard classical works, selected titles of lesser-known composers whose music deserves to be made available to a wider audience, and new editions updated to reflect the most recent findings of scholars and performers worldwide.

STUDY SCORES

BACH, Johann Sebastian (1685-1750)
MAGNIFICAT IN D, BWV 243 (NBA, ed. Dürr) SS-640

BEACH, Amy (1868-1944)
SYMPHONY IN E MINOR, Op. 32 "GAELIC" SS-063

CHADWICK, George Whitefield (1854-1931)
SYMPHONY NO. 2, Op. 21 .... SS-012
SYMPHONY NO. 3 in F SS-020

DEBUSSY, Claude Achille (1862-1918)
CHILDREN'S CORNER (orch. Caplet) SS-055
PETITE SUITE (orch. Büsser) SS-047

MACDOWELL, Edward (1861-1908)
SUITE NO. 2, Op. 48 "INDIAN" SS-470

MEDTNER, Nikolai (1880-1951)
PIANO CONCERTO NO. 1, Op. 33 .... SS-772

MUSSORGSKY, Modest (1839-1881)
PICTURES AT AN EXHIBITION, FOR WIND ORCHESTRA (orch. Simpson, ed. Reed) SS-101

RIMSKY-KORSAKOV, Nikolai (1844-1908)
SYMPHONY NO. 2, Op. 9 "ANTAR" (1897 version) SS-608

SIBELIUS, Jean (1865-1957)
SCENES HISTORIQUES, Opp. 25, 66 .... SS-659

STENHAMMAR, Wilhelm (1871-1927)
SERENADE, Op. 31 .... SS-004

STRAUSS, Johann II (1825-1899)
ROSES FROM THE SOUTH, Op. 388 (ed. McAlister) SS-624
WINE, WOMEN AND SONG, Op. 333 (ed. McAlister) SS-632

SUK, Josef (1874-1935)
FANTASICKE SCHERZO, Op. 25 .... SS-071
POHADKA LETA (A SUMMER TALE), Op. 29 .... SS-594

TCHAIKOVSKY, Peter Ilich (1840-1893)
FRANCESCA DA RIMINI, Op. 32 .... SS-039
SWAN LAKE, BALLET IN FOUR ACTS, Op. 20 (ed. Simpson) SS-616
SWAN LAKE SUITE, Op. 20a (ed. Simpson) SS-314

VOCAL SCORES

BACH, Johann Sebastian (1685-1750)
CANATA NO. 4: "CHRIST LAG IN TODES BANDEN", BWV 4 .... Z2493
CANATA NO. 31: "DIE HIMMEL LACHT, DIE ERDE JUBILIERET", BWV 31 .... Z5156
CANATA NO. 79: "GOTT DER HERR IS SONN UND SCHILD", BWV 79 .... Z2515
CANATA NO. 129: "GELOBET SEI DER HERR, MEIN GOTT", BWV 129 .... Z8425
CANATA NO. 140: "WACHET AUF, RUFT UNS DIE STIMME", BWV 140 .... Z2530
CANATA NO. 150: "NACH DIR, HERR, VERLANGET MICH", BWV 150 (ed. Torvik) Z4521
CANATA NO. 191: "GLORIA IN EXCELSIS DEO", BWV 191 (ed. Torvik) Z7520
CHRISTMAS ORATORIO, BWV 248 .... Z2487
MAGNIFICAT IN D, BWV 243 (ed. Straube) Z2488

VOCAL SCORES – CONT.

BEETHOVEN, Ludwig van (1770-1827)
CHORAL FANTASY, OP. 80 (arr. Scharwenka) Z1166
MASS IN C, OP. 86 (arr. Reinecke, ed. Torvik) Z2558
MISSA SOLEMNIS, OP. 123 (arr. Jadassohn) Z2557

BERLIOZ, Hector (1803-1869)
REQUIEM, OP. 5 (arr. Scharwenka) Z2565
TE DEUM, OP. 22 (arr. Barry) Z2568

BRAHMS, Johannes (1833-1897)
GESANG DER PARZEN, OP. 89 (arr. composer) Z2579
NÄNIE, OP. 82 (arr. composer) Z1344
SCHICKSALIED, OP. 54 (arr. composer) Z1343

BRUCKNER, Anton (1824-1896)
MASS IN E MINOR (1882 version) Z2582
PSALM 150 (arr. Hynais, ed. Torvik) Z2583
REQUIEM IN D MINOR (arr. Berberich) Z2584
TE DEUM (1886 version, arr. Schalk) Z2580

CHERUBINI, Maria Luigi (1760-1842)
REQUIEM IN C MINOR (arr. Uhlrich) Z2589
REQUIEM IN D MINOR (arr. Uhlrich) Z2588

DURANTE, Francesco (1684-1755) - mistakenly attr. PERGOLESI
MAGNIFICAT IN B-FLAT (arr. Westermann) Z2703

DVORAK, Antonin (1841-1904)
MASS IN D, OP. 86 (arr. Tours) Z2596
REQUIEM, OP. 89 (arr. composer) Z2595
STABAT MATER, OP. 58 (arr. Zubaty) Z2593
TE DEUM, OP. 103 (arr. Suk, ed. Simpson) Z2594

ELGAR, Edward (1865-1934)
THE MUSIC MAKERS, OP. 69 .... Z0586

FAURE, Gabriel (1845-1924)
REQUIEM, OP. 48 (1900 version, arr. Roger-Ducasse) Z2598

GOUNOD, Charles (1818-1893)
MESSE SOLENNELLE DE STE. CECEILE (arr. Barnby) Z2607
ROMEO ET JULIETTE, CHORUS SCORE (arr. Salomon) Z3029

HANDEL, George Frideric (1685-1759)
CHANDOS ANTHEM IX: "O PRAISE THE LORD WITH ONE CONSENT", HWV 254 (arr. Päsler, ed. Seiffert) ... Z5139
JUDAS MACCABAEUS, HWV 63 .... Z2615

MAHLER, Gustav (1860-1911)
SYMPHONY NO. 8 (arr. Wöss) Z6070

MENDELSSOHN, Felix (1809-1847)
ELIJAH OP. 70 (arr. Kretzschmar) Z2659
ST. PAUL, OP. 36 (arr. Horn, ed. Dörffel) Z2661

MOZART, Wolfgang Amadeus (1756-1791)
BENEDICTUS SIT DEUS, K. 117/66A (arr. Messner) Z2676
MASS IN C MINOR, K. 427 (arr. Schmitt) Z2699
MASS IN C, K. 317 "CORONATION" (arr. Taubmann) Z2694
MISSA BREVIS IN D. K. 194 (arr. Trexler, ed. Torvik) Z2685
REGINA COELI, K. 276 (arr. Scheel) Z2692
REQUIEM, K. 626 (Süssmayr completion, arr. Brissler) Z2670
TE DEUM, K. 141 (arr. Gleichauf, ed. Torvik) Z2678
VENI SANCTE SPIRITUS, K. 47 (arr. Müller) Z2674
VESPERAE SOLENNES DE CONFESSORE, K. 339 (arr. Fuller-Maitland) Z2697

VOCAL SCORES - CONT.

PURCELL, Henry (1659-1695)
Dido & Aeneas, Z. 626 (arr. Cummings) Z2328

SAINT-SAENS, Camille (1835-1921)
Oratorio de Noel, Op. 12 (arr. Gigout) Z2710

SCHUBERT, Franz Peter (1797-1828)
Mass in G, D. 167 (arr. Spiro) Z2716
Mass in E-flat, D. 950 (arr. Spengel) Z2718
Stabat Mater, D. 353 (arr. Gohler) Z2720

SCHUMANN, Robert (1810-1856)
Requiem, Op. 148 (arr. composer, ed. Torvik) Z7761

VIVALDI, Antonio (1678-1741)
Credo, RV 591 (arr. Westermann) Z2734
Gloria, RV 589 (arr. Westermann) Z2732
Magnificat, RV 610-611 (arr. Westermann) Z2733

www.ingramcontent.com/pod-product-compliance
Lightning Source LLC
Chambersburg PA
CBHW081026040426

42444CB00014B/3372